We Want Watermelon

Lada Kratky
Illustrations by Renate Lohmann

HAMPTON-BROWN

This is the way
we wash the watermelon.

This is the way
we carry the watermelon.

This is the way
we pull the watermelon.

This is the way
we push the watermelon.

This is the way
we lift the watermelon.

This is the way
we eat the watermelon.